A DAY IN AN ECOSYSTEM

24 HOURS IN A TROPICAL RAIN FOREST

VIRGINIA SCHOMP

Cavendish Square
New York

Published in 2014 by Cavendish Square Publishing, LLC
303 Park Avenue South, Suite 1247, New York, NY 10010

First Edition

Website: cavendishsq.com

This publication represents the opinions and views of the author based on his or her personal experience, knowledge, and research. The information in this book serves as a general guide only. The author and publisher have used their best efforts in preparing this book and disclaim liability rising directly or indirectly from the use and application of this book.

CPSIA Compliance Information: Batch #WS13CSQ

All websites were available and accurate when this book was sent to press.

Library of Congress Cataloging-in-Publication Data
Schomp, Virginia.
24 hours in a tropical rain forest / Virginia Schomp.
p. cm. — (a day in an ecosystem)
Includes bibliographical references and index.
Summary: "Take a look at what takes place within a 24-hour period in a tropical rain forest. Learn firsthand about the features, plant life, and animals of the habitat"—Provided by publisher.
ISBN 978-1-60870-895-6 (hardcover) ISBN 978-1-62712-068-5 (paperback)
ISBN 978-1-60870-902-1 (ebook)
1. Rain forest ecology—Juvenile literature. I. Title. II. Title: Twenty four hours in a tropical rain forest.
QH541.5.R27S37 2013
577.34—dc23

Editor: Peter Mavrikis
Art Director: Anahid Hamparian
Series Designer: Kay Petronio
Photo research by Alison Morretta

Printed in the United States of America

CONTENTS

DAWN

A NEW DAY is beginning—but where is the sun? You stand in a dark green world, surrounded by towering trees. Look up! High above your head, leafy branches shut out the sky. Listen! All around you, insects hum and click and whine. Birds screech and squawk. Tree frogs chirp. Howler monkeys make their strange roaring sound. The whole noisy chorus is greeting the dawn in the Amazon **rain forest**.

You can probably guess how rain forests got their name. They are *forests* that grow in places where there is a lot of *rain.* These forests get at least 100 inches (254 centimeters) of rain a year. In some rain forests, it rains almost every day.

Do you like warm weather? If so, you will really like it here. The Amazon is a **tropical** rain forest. It grows in the tropics, near the earth's **equator**. In the tropics, it is warm all year round.

Plants and animals thrive in the warm, wet tropics. Tropical rain forests

◀ You would have to climb high in the mountains of Brazil to get this bird's-eye view of dawn in the Amazon rain forest.

A satellite photo of South America and the Amazon rain forest

THE LARGEST RAIN FOREST

The Amazon is the largest rain forest in the world. It covers about 2.5 million square miles (6.5 million square kilometers) in the northern part of South America. How big is that? If this super-sized forest were a country, it would be the seventh-largest country on earth.

cover only a small part of the earth, but they hold more than *half* of the world's plant and animal **species**. Can you picture a patch of rain forest about the size of a baseball diamond? That small patch may hold 300 different kinds of trees. Now think of just one tree in that forest. It may be home to more than 1,500 types of insects!

Thousands of different types of plants grow in the rain forest, including this colorful bromeliad (broh-MEE-lee-ad).

No rain forest has more species than the Amazon. Thousands of different kinds of plants live here. So do millions of different animals. Let's take a walk and find out how all these living things get along in their wild green world.

GREEN GIANTS

Tropical rain forests grow in warm places. Temperate rain forests grow where it is cool. Some of the world's tallest trees are found in temperate forests. One redwood in California's Redwood National Forest is nearly 380 feet (116 meters) tall. That is seven stories taller than the Statue of Liberty!

MORNING

DRIP-DRIP-SPLAT! It rained during the night. Water is trickling down the branches and dripping off the leaves. You may want to wear rubber boots on your hike through the rain forest. Remember your hat and raincoat, too. The Amazon gets up to 120 inches (300 centimeters) of rain a year. That is almost twice as much as the rainiest cities in Canada or the United States.

Some days are wetter than others. Like all rain forests, the Amazon has a rainy season and a short dry season. The rainy season brings heavy rains every day. In the dry season, the skies are less cloudy, but there are still light showers from time to time.

All that rain keeps the rain forest lush and green. Most of the trees here are evergreens. They keep their leaves all through the year. No matter what season it is, they keep growing. In fact, the Amazon gets

Raindrops drip from the tips of evergreen leaves in the Amazon rain forest.

even *greener* during the dry season, when the extra sunlight helps the trees sprout new leaves.

Plants need more than just water to live. They also need light. And in a place as crowded as the rain forest, they have to fight for every drop of sun.

The tropical rain forest is made up of four layers. The top layer is called the **upper canopy**. This is where the tops of the tallest trees stick out above the rest of the forest. They are the winners in the battle for sunlight.

Only a small amount of sunlight filters down through the dense rain forest canopy.

Below the upper canopy is the **canopy**. The trees in this layer may have just a few low branches or none at all. At the top, the branches spread out to form a leafy green roof over the forest.

Between the canopy and the ground is the **understory**. The upper layers trap most of the sunlight, so it is darker down here. Shrubs and small trees grow in the shadows. Some of the trees are naturally small. Others are young canopy trees. These **saplings** sprouted from seeds. They grew a few feet and stopped. Now they sit in the dim forest, waiting for a chance to shoot up toward the light.

The bottom layer of the rain forest is the **forest floor**. Few green plants grow here, because there is so little light. The ground is mostly bare, except for a jumble of fallen branches and leaves.

Take a close look at those dead branches. Tiny red mushrooms are sprouting from the

READY, SET, GROW!

When a tree falls in the rain forest, light streams down through the gap in the canopy. Small saplings start to grow. The young trees race to see which will reach the top first. In just a few years, the winner spreads out its branches and the forest becomes dark once again.

Bracket fungus looks like shelves growing out from the sides of a tree.

wood. Mushrooms are a kind of **fungus**. Fungi feed on the wood and leaves on the forest floor. They break up the tough vegetation into smaller parts. The **nutrients** return to the soil, where they feed the roots of living plants. You can see why fungi are sometimes called the "recyclers" of the rain forest.

Millions of small creatures help run the "recycling center." Ants, beetles, termites, and earthworms creep and crawl over the dark, damp forest floor. They chew up the rotting wood and leaves. The food passes through their bodies. It comes out the other end in a form that plants can use as food. These busy little creatures are cleaning up the forest floor and making plant food at the same time!

The forest floor is home to many kinds of larger creatures, too. Piglike peccaries wander about, digging for roots. Tapirs use their rubbery snouts to sniff out leaves, grasses, and fruits. Ring-tailed coatis roam the forest in bands. They are searching for insects, mice, and frogs to eat. No food on the ground? No problem. The coatis just scoot up a tree for their breakfast.

Watch your step! You almost tripped over those roots. The roots of rain forest trees spread out close to the surface, where most of the plant food is found. The tallest trees have enormous roots called **buttresses**. Buttress roots bend like crooked knees above the ground. They help the trees take in air and food. They also keep trees with shallow roots from falling over in the thin, wet soil.

Shallow roots and buttresses are **adaptations**. Adaptations are ways that living things change to fit in with their surroundings. The plants all around you have adapted to survive in the different layers of the rain forest.

Take a look at the plant leaves. Some of them are as big as dinner

Buttress roots help support tall trees in the shallow rain forest soil.

Busy leaf-cutter ants

THE SMALLEST FARMERS

Some rain forest insects grow their own food. Leaf-cutter ants carry leaves back to their gardens under the ground. The gardens are filled with a kind of fungus that grows only in the Amazon. The fungi eat the leaves—and the ants eat the fungi.

plates. These jumbo leaves are an adaptation to the low light in the understory. They help the plants capture as much light as possible.

Now look at the shape of the leaves. They come to a point at the tip. These "drip tips" help leaves dry off quickly after a rain shower. That keeps them free of the fungi and mold that like to grow on warm, wet surfaces.

Trees can grow toward the sun. But what about smaller plants? How do they survive beneath the canopy? Some plants have adapted to life in the shade. Others find ways to rise up into the light.

Some rain forest plants grow on tree branches to get closer to the sunlight.

Colorful **orchids** bloom on the branch of a tall tree. Ferns and mosses sprout in nooks where the branches meet the trunk. All these small plants are **epiphytes**. Epiphytes are also called "air plants." They grow on other plants instead of in the ground. As the tree grows, it lifts the hitchhiking plants toward the sunny canopy.

Tall trees are also home to lots of vines. You can see them coiling around the trunks and hanging from the branches. Some of the vines started out as shrubs in the understory. They wound themselves around a nearby tree and grew up toward the light. As vines grow, they help themselves to the tree's light and water.

Strangler vines are especially greedy. These thick vines grow from seeds dropped on a branch by a bird or monkey. When the seeds sprout, they send roots down to the ground. They send branches up toward the canopy. Over time, the roots and branches surround the tree, cutting off all the sunlight. The tree dies and rots away. The strangler vine lives on. It looks like a big hollow tree growing in the forest.

The water-holding "tank" of an epiphyte

LIVING WATER TANKS

Epiphytes get their water from rain. But what happens when the rains stop? Many air plants have long, curved leaves arranged like a cup. Rainwater collects in the plant's "water tank." A large air plant can store up to 2 gallons (7.5 liters) of water to drink during the dry season.

AFTERNOON

IT IS NOON. The sun is high in the sky, but the world around you is still dark and gloomy. Even in the shade, it is hot. The temperature in the Amazon stays at around 80 degrees Fahrenheit (27 degrees Celsius) all through the year. The high **humidity** makes it seem even hotter. There is so much water in the air that it feels like you are standing in a steamy bathroom after a long, hot shower.

Why is the Amazon so wet? About half of the rain comes from moist winds blowing in from the Atlantic Ocean. Rain forests also make their own rain. The plants soak up water. They release some of that water through tiny holes in their leaves. The evaporating water rises into the air and forms clouds. Rain falls from the clouds—and the cycle starts all over again.

◀ Even in the shade, afternoons are hot and steamy in the tropical rain forest.

A cloud forest in Peru

LIFE IN THE CLOUDS

Cloud forests are rain forests that grow in the mountains. The tops of the trees disappear into the mist and clouds. The branches are covered with air plants. These plants get all the water they need from the moisture in the cool, damp mountain air.

With so much rain, the animals here never go thirsty. But that does not mean their lives are one long vacation. Millions of different kinds of creatures live in the Amazon. They all need food to survive. Plant-eaters have to find their favorite plants to eat. **Predators** must hunt and catch their **prey**.

A small reddish brown bird pecks through the leaves on the forest floor. It is an antbird, looking for insects to eat. Some antbirds spend their days following after army ants. The ants swarm over the ground in huge hunting parties. The birds dart out and catch insects and spiders that run away from the fierce, hungry ants.

Trogons live higher up, in the understory. See that flash of shiny red and blue? A blue-crowned trogon is inspecting a cluster of figs. The bird picks a fig and carries it back to a perch to eat.

The trogon shares the understory with the hoatzin. This wacky-looking bird has a bare blue face and a crown of spiky gold feathers. Even its diet is strange. Nearly all of the plant-eating birds of the rain forest feed on fruits, seeds, and **nectar**. The hoatzin munches on leaves.

Leaves are hard on the stomach. How does the hoatzin deal with its tough, stringy diet? It has an unusual way of digesting food. Its meals

One scientist has described the hoatzin as a "punk rock chicken."

go into a large pouch in its body. The pouch is filled with **bacteria**. The bacteria break down the plant material into small parts. By the time the food gets to the bird's stomach, it is a nutritious mush.

The hoatzin's food pouch is an adaptation to its tropical home. This bird never has to look far for a meal. In the Amazon, leaves are easy to find!

Look around and you will see other ways birds have adapted to life in the tropical rain forest. The trogon's wings have special slots. The slots let the bird hover over a branch as it searches for food. The antbird has long claws and toes. It can sit "sideways" on a tree trunk. Perched close to the ground, it can keep a close eye on ant swarms—and keep just out of reach of the biting ants.

The antbird also has a kind of adaptation called **camouflage**. Its reddish brown feathers blend in with the fallen leaves. That helps this little bird hide from predators on the forest floor.

Other rain forest creatures have their own amazing adaptations. Pythons and boa constrictors have heat detectors on their snouts. The snakes use their sensors to "see" their warm-blooded prey in the dark. The giant anteater has a super-strong sense of smell. It can sniff out ants and termites. It rips open the anthills and termite mounds with its powerful claws. *Slurp!* The anteater's long, sticky tongue is perfect for lapping up tiny insects.

Some adaptations help animals move around in the forest. Look up and you will see a group of howler monkeys scrambling around in the trees. These noisy monkeys have **prehensile** tails. They use their grasping tails like an extra hand when they climb. They can even hang by their tails. That leaves their hands free for eating.

A howler monkey scurries past a lump hanging from a branch. From where you are standing, it looks like a big furry fruit. Then it starts to move. Slowly. Very . . . very . . . s-l-o-w-l-y. The strange-looking lump is a tree sloth, one of the slowest creatures on earth.

Sloths do not have prehensile tails. How do they keep their grip up in the trees? They have long curved claws for hanging on to the trunks and branches. They can even hold on when they are asleep. Tree sloths spend so much time sleeping that a tiny green plantlike organism called **algae** may grow on their fur.

A well-camouflaged bushmaster

HIDING IN PLAIN SIGHT

Camouflage can help an animal hide from hungry hunters. But watch out! This trick of nature works for predators, too. You might not notice this brown-and-black bushmaster on the forest floor. The snake is waiting for a bird or mouse to wander by. With a bite of its long fangs, it will inject deadly **venom** into its prey.

These noisy red howler monkeys will spend their whole lives in the treetops.

You will hardly ever see a sloth down on the ground. You will never find an antbird up in the canopy. Each creature has its own special place in the rain forest. Scientists call that place its **niche**.

A niche means the part of the forest where the animal lives. It also includes the special way the animal lives in that place. Some animals feed on a particular plant or part of a plant. Others eat a certain kind of bug. Some roam the forest by day, while others come out at night.

All these different ways of life make it possible for many different species to live together in the tropical rain forest. You might think of

The sloth's long hooked claws are the perfect tools for hanging around in the canopy.

the forest like a giant apartment building. All the people live in their own apartments. They eat in separate cafeterias. They go to work and school at different times of the day. You could live in the building your whole life and never even meet the person who lives right next door!

Listen! Do you hear that loud clapping sound? A red-billed ground cuckoo is snapping its beak. The cuckoo lives on the rain forest floor. It has a clever way of getting fruit from the branches above. The bird follows a group of golden lion tamarins as they swing through the trees. The monkeys are picking fruit. One of them drops a half-eaten berry. In a flash, the cuckoo gobbles it up.

Like the ground cuckoo and tamarin, many rain forest species depend on other species for their survival. Sometimes the connection is a one-way street. The cuckoo gets a sweet fruit. The tamarin does not lose anything—but it does not gain anything either. Other times, the relationship is good for one side and bad for the other. Do you see that hollow tree? It is really a strangler vine. The vine killed the tree that it used to climb up to the canopy.

Most often, the connection between species is good for both sides. Remember the air plants? A host of creatures depend on the water stored in the plants' water tanks. Bacteria and algae grow in the miniature pools. These tiny living things become food for insects. Frogs, birds, and monkeys stop by to sip the water and eat the insects. Some frogs lay their eggs in the water. The egg cases, animal droppings, and bodies of dead insects sink to the bottom of the water. They make a nutritious brown "soup" that helps feed the air plant.

An ant inside the hollow stem of an ant plant

ANTS TO THE RESCUE

Ants and ant plants take care of each other. The plants make a home for ants in their trunks, stems, or leaves. They even produce special sugars and oils to feed their ant colony. In return, the ants swarm out to sting any animal that tries to munch on the plant.

EVENING

YOU HEAR the rumble of thunder. The forest gets even darker than before. With a sudden *whoosh*, the rain comes pounding down. The storm lasts just a few minutes. Then it stops as quickly as it started.

Sunbeams peek through the canopy up ahead. Follow the path and you will come to a stream tumbling over big black rocks. The sunlit banks of the stream are a jungle of shrubs, saplings, and vines.

Thousands of streams and rivers flow through the Amazon rain forest. Some of the rivers are fast and wild. Others wander in lazy loops through the forest. The waters may be clear, or they may look like a chocolate milkshake. The brownish water carries bits of rock and dirt washed from the mountains and highlands. This **sediment** is rich in minerals. When the rivers flood, they add nutrients to the forest soil.

The greatest of all the rivers is the one that gave this forest its name. The Amazon River starts high in the Andes Mountains of Peru. It winds

A waterfall carries nutrient-rich soil to the lowlands of the Amazon rain forest.

Striped fish in the Amazon River

A FISHY FOREST

During the rainy season in the Amazon rain forest, rivers overflow. Large areas of the forest are flooded for months at a time. Fish swim among the trees. They feast on the fruits that fall into the water. When they swim on, their poop helps spread the trees' seeds through the forest.

its way through the rain forest, collecting water from the smaller streams and rivers. It carries its waters all the way to the Atlantic Ocean on the coast of Brazil.

Your hike has made you hot and sweaty. You might think about taking a swim. Think again! The lakes, streams, and rivers of the rain forest are home to all kinds of creatures. Most of them will not bother you—but some can be nasty.

More than three thousand kinds of fish live in the Amazon region. Many of the fish are plant-eaters. The tambaqui eats fruits and seeds that fall into the water. This large fish has strong teeth for grinding up its favorite food—hard rubber tree seeds.

Most piranhas feed on fruits and seeds, too. Not the red-bellied piranha! This fierce fish uses its razor-sharp teeth to attack other fish, birds, frogs, and even larger animals. The piranha is small. It can only bite off a tiny bit at a time. But

The red-bellied piranha is a small fish with a powerful bite.

these fish hunt in packs. A pack of hungry piranhas can strip the flesh from a large animal in just a few minutes.

The rivers and swamps are also home to anacondas. These huge snakes can grow more than 30 feet (9 meters) long. Anacondas eat fish, frogs, turtles, and large animals such as deer and monkeys. The snake coils itself around its victim. It squeezes until the animal cannot breathe. Then it swallows its prey whole.

Anacondas are shy around people. The Amazon River dolphin may swim right up to say hello. This curious dolphin is gray or bubble-gum pink. It uses sound to hunt for fish, crabs, and turtles in the muddy river waters. During

Sediments in the Amazon River can make pink river dolphins look orange.

the rainy season, dolphins head for the flooded forest. Their skinny beak, bendy neck, and large flippers help them steer through the trees and pluck fish from the branches.

In some parts of the Amazon, you can walk for days and never see another person. It is hard to believe that the forest is home to more than 20 million people. Most of the people live in towns and cities near the larger rivers. About half a million live in villages deep in the rain forest.

The native peoples of the forest belong to many different tribal groups. A few tribes have had no contact with the outside world. The people of these tribes live just like their great-great-grandparents did long ago. Other tribes know about the world outside the forest. They follow the old ways, with a few modern touches.

Walk back along the path and you will come to a Kayapo village. You see a large circle of houses. The Kayapo build their houses from branches woven together and covered with mud. **Thatch** roofs keep the insides cool and dry. Each house holds a large family. A grandmother and grandfather share their home with their daughters, their daughters' husbands, and their grandchildren.

"**Akati mêtch**! Good day!" A group of children greet you. Some of them are dressed in shorts just like yours. Others have colorful bands of cloth tied around the waist and draped across the chest. The children and grown-ups wear beaded necklaces, armbands, and wristbands. Their

During special ceremonies, Kayapo hunters still use the traditional spears and arrows of their ancestors.

bodies are decorated with red and black paint. The designs tell a story of each person's place in the Kayapo family.

It is almost time for the evening meal. Women are baking tambaqui fish in the coals of the cooking fires. Rice and beans bubble in a modern metal cook pot. Kayapo women not only cook the food—they also raise the crops. Their special way of farming gets the most from the soil. It also helps keep the rain forest healthy.

First, the men cut down a few trees to let in the light. They burn the trees and fertilize the soil with the ashes. Then the women plant the seeds for a variety of fruits and vegetables. Some of the Kayapo's favorite foods are yams, sugar cane, maize (corn), bananas, melons, and a potato-like root called manioc. The crops are planted in carefully planned circles. Tall plants shield smaller ones from the scorching sun. Plants with large leaves protect the soil from heavy rains.

After a few years, the soil begins to wear out. The men clear space for new gardens. But the older patches are not abandoned. Women gather wild plants from the forest. These hardy plants grow quickly in the old clearings. They provide the people with nuts, seeds, berries, and medicines. The half-wild gardens also offer food and shelter to birds and animals.

The men of the village are in charge of getting meat for their families. They fish in the streams and rivers. They hunt in the forest. In the past, Kayapo hunters used spears, bows and arrows, and poison darts. Today most of the men hunt with rifles. When a lucky man catches a big deer or anteater, he shares the meat with the rest of the village.

A golden poison dart frog

SMALL BUT DEADLY

The poison dart frog is cute and colorful. It is also one of the deadliest animals in the rain forest. The skin of this little frog contains a powerful poison. The poison comes from chemicals in the ants the frog eats. Some native peoples use the frog's poison to coat the tips of hunting darts and arrows.

NIGHT

THERE IS another visitor in the Kayapo village. It is a plant scientist from a city in Peru. For many years, the peoples of the rain forest have used plants to treat sickness. Scientists come here to learn about these plants. They take leaves, bark, seeds, and roots to study in their labs back home.

This work has led to important discoveries. One-fourth of all the medicines we use today came from rain forest plants. These drugs help us in many ways. They treat everything from toothaches to cancer. It is no wonder the rain forest has been called "nature's medicine chest."

It is not easy learning about life in the rain forest. Most of the plants and animals live way up in the canopy. How do you study a place that is so hard to reach?

 Night falls over the tall trees of the Amazon rain forest.

HELPFUL POISONS

Why would a plant produce harmful chemicals? To make sure it does not become a plant-eater's lunch! Some plant poisons make good medicines. A tiny drop can be safe for a sick person to take—and deadly for the germs that are making the person sick.

Researchers have found a way. They have built platforms in tall trees. The platforms are connected by walkways. These sky-scraping bridges let people explore the world above the forest floor.

Are you ready to walk in the treetops? You must follow the scientist up the winding stairs inside a wooden tower. The higher you climb, the more crowded the forest gets. The bare trunks give way to leafy branches. The trunks and branches are smothered with vines, mosses, and air plants.

This walkway was built so that scientists could study plant and animal life in the canopy.

At last, you reach the top. You step out onto the walkway. The rain forest stretches out beneath your feet. It looks like a giant green blanket dotted with brightly colored flowers.

You are not the only one who has seen all the flowers. Hummingbirds are zipping from blossom to blossom. They use their long bills to suck up the nectar deep inside tube-shaped flowers. The little birds hover like helicopters as they feed. Can you hear the *buzz*? That is the sound of a hummingbird's wings sweeping rapidly back and forth.

Other canopy birds feed on fruit or flesh. Here comes a noisy flock of parrots. These colorful birds use their strong, curved beaks to crack open shells and pluck out the fruit inside.

A toucan settles on a nearby branch. Its beak looks like a weird rainbow-colored banana. The toucan picks a berry and tosses it in the air. It tilts back its head and swallows the fruit whole.

PETAL POWER

Flowers are not just pretty to look at. They make the seeds that grow into new plants. To make seeds, a plant needs **pollen** from another plant of the same species. Insects, birds, and bats carry the powdery pollen from flower to flower. Plants use colors, smells, shapes, oils, and nectar to attract these helpful creatures.

The toucan's colors act as camouflage in the bright, flowering canopy.

Toucans also may eat eggs, insects, and small snakes or birds.

The king of the birds is the harpy eagle. This large, fearsome hunter builds its nest in the upper canopy. It sits silently for hours, waiting for a large animal to appear. The eagle spots a sloth slowly climbing a tree. It dives down and grabs its prey with its long, hooked claws.

A troop of spider monkeys screech when the eagle attacks. Soon the danger is past, and the monkeys get back to their favorite activity—eating figs and other sweet fruits. There is plenty of food in the canopy for other monkeys, too. Squirrel monkeys leap from tree to tree, gathering fruits and insects. Marmosets chew holes into tree trunks and lap up the sticky gum and sap.

Night falls quickly in the rain forest. Soon the world below the canopy is as black as ink. Daytime creatures have settled into their nests and sleeping perches. It is time for the **nocturnal** animals to come out.

Creak! Gurgle! Chirp! Croak! Thousands of frogs raise their voices. They are calling for a mate. The darkness helps hide the frogs from hungry predators. It also brings out the moths, mosquitoes, and other insects they like to eat.

Night is the time for bats, too. There are almost a thousand different types of bats in the Amazon. The vampire bat's favorite food is blood. Other bats may eat insects, small birds, and **rodents**. Still others feed on fruit or nectar.

While the bats glide through the canopy, hunters are prowling down below. A tarantula hides in the underbrush. The hairs on this big spider's legs can feel the vibrations when a mouse passes by. *Zap!* The spider darts out and injects venom into its prey.

The top predator in the rain forest is the jaguar. This powerful cat hunts monkeys, sloths, and other large animals. The jaguar also likes fish. It lies on a low branch over a stream and scoops out the fish with its paws.

A jaguar stalks silently through the dark forest, listening for its prey.

You light a lantern. Yikes! Something is staring right at you! No need to worry. It is just a spectacled owl, on the lookout for mice and insects. Like many nocturnal animals, owls have large eyes that are specially designed to see in the dark.

Owls are one small part of a very important **ecosystem**. Why are tropical rain forests so important? They hold more kinds of plants and animals than any other place on earth. They provide wood, medicines, fruits, nuts, spices, and other valuable products. The trees help recycle the world's water. They help clean the air that we breathe.

But the rain forests are in trouble. Settlers have cleared huge areas to make way for homes and farms. Logging companies have cut down billions of trees. Miners and oil companies have damaged the land and polluted the water.

What happens when a part of the rain forest is destroyed? The creatures that lived there lose their homes and their food. Plants and animals that depended on those creatures suffer, too. Some species become **extinct**. Extinction means that the last member of the species has died. The plant or animal is lost forever.

This owl gets its name from the white markings that make it look like it is wearing "spectacles," or eyeglasses.

The good news is that many people are trying to save the rain forests. Governments have set aside land for parks, where the plants and animals are protected. Conservation groups are working with loggers and miners. They are finding ways to take out trees and other products without damaging the whole forest.

Some of the best conservation projects involve local tribes such as the Kayapo. These peoples have lived in the forests for thousands of years. They know how to harvest the riches of the land without destroying it. If we can learn from their wisdom, these wonderful wild places will be with us for many years to come.

More than half of the world's tropical rain forests have been cut down.

WHERE ARE THE TROPICAL RAIN FORESTS?

ARCTIC OCEAN

NORTH AMERICA

EUROPE

ASIA

PACIFIC OCEAN

AFRICA

PACIFIC OCEAN

Equator

Amazon

ATLANTIC OCEAN

INDIAN OCEAN

SOUTH AMERICA

AUSTRALIA

Equator

Amazon

SOUTH AMERICA

SOUTHERN OCEAN

Rain forests cover about 6 percent of the world's land surface. This map shows the location of the main rain forest areas.

FAST FACTS ABOUT THE AMAZON RAIN FOREST

SIZE: About 2.5 million square miles (6.5 million square kilometers).

LOCATION: The Amazon rain forest is located in northern South America. More than half of the forest is in Brazil. The rest extends into eight other countries: Bolivia, Peru, Ecuador, Colombia, Venezuela, Guyana, Suriname, and French Guiana.

LAND SURFACES: The rain forest occupies a large basin, or lowland area. It is bounded by the Andes Mountains to the west, the Guiana Highlands to the north, and the Brazilian Highlands to the southeast.

TEMPERATURES: Average annual temperature is 80°F (27°C).

RAINFALL: From about 80 to 120 inches (200 to 300 centimeters) a year. There is a long rainy season and a short dry season. The seasons stop and start at different times in different parts of the forest.

MAJOR WATER SOURCES: The Amazon River is at least 4,000 miles (6,400 kilometers) long. It is the world's second-longest river, after the Nile River in Africa. More than 1,000 other rivers flow through the Amazon, including the Madeira, Purus, Japurá, Tocantins, Juruá, Rio Negro, and Xingu.

PLANTS: At least 40,000 species of plants, including trees, vines, lianas (thick climbing vines), shrubs, orchids, bromeliads, ferns, and mosses.

ANIMALS: Millions of species of animals. *Mammals* include jaguars, sloths, anteaters, howler monkeys, spider monkeys, squirrel monkeys, tamarins, tapirs, capybaras, peccaries, coatis, opossums, red deer, manatees, and Amazon river dolphins. *Birds* include parrots, macaws, toucans, trogons, antbirds, ground cuckoos, hoatzins, owls, hawks, and harpy eagles. *Reptiles* include coral snakes, boa constrictors, pythons, bushmasters, anacondas, caimans, lizards, and turtles. *Amphibians* include poison dart frogs (also called poison arrow frogs), monkey frogs, and leaf toads. *Invertebrates* include tarantulas, slugs, snails, earthworms, and insects such as butterflies, bees, mosquitoes, grasshoppers, ants, termites, and beetles. *Fish* include catfish, piranhas, tambaqui, pirarucu, electric eels, and stingrays.

POPULATION: About 20 million to 30 million people. More than 70 percent live in large towns and cities. There are about 500,000 native peoples belonging to hundreds of different tribes, including the Kayapo, Yanomami, Xingu, Aguaruna, and Huaorani.

GLOSSARY

adaptations—Ways in which living things adapt, or change to survive under the conditions in a certain environment.

akati mêtch **(ah-kah-tee MAYTCH)**—"Hello" or "good day" in the language of the Kayapo people.

algae (AL-jee)—Tiny plantlike organisms made of one or more cells.

bacteria (back-TEER-ee-uh)—Simple living things made up of just one cell, which are usually too small to see without a microscope.

buttresses—Large roots that grow above the ground on all sides of a tall tree.

camouflage (KAM-uh-flaj)—Coloring or other physical features that help living things blend in with their surroundings, hiding them from other animals.

canopy—The second-highest layer of the tropical rain forest. The trees in this layer may be 60 to 90 feet (18 to 27 meters) tall.

ecosystem—An area that is home to a particular community of plants and animals, which are specially suited to living in that environment. An ecosystem includes all the living things of the area plus all the nonliving things, such as the temperature, water, and rocks.

epiphytes (EH-puh-fîtes)—Plants that grow on other plants, instead of in the ground. Epiphytes are also called air plants.

equator—An imaginary line around the middle of the earth.

extinct—No longer existing. A plant or an animal is extinct when every one of its kind has died.

forest floor—The bottom layer of the rain forest.

fungus (FUN-gus)—A small plantlike organism such as a mushroom, which feeds on living and dead plants and animals. The word for more than one fungus is *fungi* (FUN-jee).

humidity—The amount of water vapor in the air.

nectar—A sweet liquid made by flowers.

niche (nitch)—The special habitat of a species. Niche includes the place where the plant or animal lives and the way it survives in that place.

nocturnal—Active mainly at night.

nutrients (NOO-tree-uhnts)—Substances that are taken in by plants and animals to help them live and grow.

orchids (OR-kudz)—Colorful tropical plants. Most orchids are epiphytes.

pollen—A powder produced by flowers. Pollen must be carried from one plant to another so that plants can make seeds.

predators—Animals that hunt and kill other animals for food.

prehensile (pree-HEN-sul)—Adapted for grasping an object, especially by wrapping around it. Many monkeys have prehensile tails.

prey—Animals that are hunted by predators.

rain forest—A woodland that gets at least 100 inches (254 centimeters) of rain throughout the year and has mostly tall broad-leafed evergreen trees.

rodents—Small animals with big front teeth for gnawing. Mice and rats are rodents.

saplings—Young trees.

sediment—Tiny bits of rock, dirt, and other materials carried by water.

species (SPEE-sheez)—Specific types of plants and animals.

thatch—A roofing material made of dried leaves or straw.

tropical—Found in the tropics, the warm region just north and south of the earth's equator.

understory—The layer between the canopy and the forest floor. The shrubs and small trees may be less than 12 feet (3.7 meters) tall.

upper canopy—The top layer of the tropical rain forest, where the trees reach as high as 200 feet (60 meters) above the ground.

venom—The poison of some snakes, spiders, and other animals.

FIND OUT MORE

Books

Green, Jen. *Rain Forest Extremes*. New York: Crabtree, 2009.

Simon, Seymour. *Tropical Rainforests*. New York: Smithsonian, 2010.

Tagliaferro, Linda. *Explore the Tropical Rain Forest*. Mankato, MN: Capstone Press, 2007.

Vogt, Richard C. *Rain Forests*. New York: Simon & Schuster Books for Young Readers, 2009.

Watson, Galadriel. *The Amazon Rain Forest: The Largest Rain Forest in the World*. New York: Weigl Publishers, 2005.

Websites

Enchanted Learning: All about Rainforests

www.enchantedlearning.com/subjects/rainforest

This Enchanted Learning site has information and activity sheets for learning about rain forests and the animals that live there.

Enter Amazonia

www.pbs.org/journeyintoamazonia/enter.html

This PBS site takes you on a journey to the Amazon rain forest. Click on the "Play Amazon Explorer" link for an interesting interactive game.

Rainforest Heroes

http://rainforestheroes.ran.org/help-save-rainforests/7-steps-kids-can-take/

Check out the seven steps kids can take to help save the rain forests.

Tropical Rainforests

http://kids.mongabay.com/

This site has lots of good information for school reports. It covers topics including the plants, animals, and people of the rain forests.

INDEX

Page numbers in **boldface** are illustrations.

ABOUT THE AUTHOR

VIRGINIA SCHOMP has written more than eighty books for young readers on topics including dinosaurs, dolphins, world history, American history, myths, and legends. She lives among the tall pines of New York's Catskill Mountain region. When she is not writing books, she enjoys hiking, gardening, baking (and eating!) cookies, watching old movies and new anime, and, of course, reading, reading, and reading.

PHOTO CREDITS